TABLE OF CONTENT

Introduction by CEO Insider Patrick Janin My Years of Stressful Vacations 02

Vacation Stress Triggers: Why We Don't Walk Away from Work 06

Planning Your Vacation Benefits the Entire Office 10

Set Your Dates Beyond Booking a Flight.. 15

Your Mindset About Travel Does Matter 20

Talk About Your Trip, With Everyone... 23

At All Times Delegate to Your Assistant 28

The Details of Delegating Before You Travel 32

The Two Weeks Before You Leave.. 36

What to Do Two Days Before You Fly 40

Benefits of Truly Walking Away from Work................................... 44

Your Triumphant Return to Work: How to Stay Stress-Free 47

Are You Ready for a Vacation? Try Our Scorecard!.......................... 51

Where to Take Your Getaway 59

Sources 63

CHAPTER 1

My Years of STRESSFUL VACATIONS

As an executive you've been there.

In the midst of planning a family vacation or getaway with your significant other, the stress of booking flights, organizing the office, rearranging meeting, and preparing overtakes the potential joy of travel.

Over days, and sometimes weeks, you half-heartedly field questions about possible flights and picking this restaurant or that. Your lackluster answers already indicate the real direction this trip is taking – towards cancellation. Stressors at work build, as does the frustration at home. And all over what's supposed to be a positive experience.

Eventually, you scrap the entire trip or scale back the duration and adventure of travel. Very likely, the next conversation about taking a vacation doesn't even get off the ground.

CHAPTER 2

Vacation Stress Triggers:
WHY WE DON'T WALK AWAY FROM WORK

In total, Americans aren't using half (54% to be exact) of their hard-earned vacation days each year. The statistics around the use of vacation days in Europe, Australia, and Asia are better, but studies have revealed that workers around the world are taking less time off than ever before.

My earlier book, *Overworked*, discusses trends in CEO and entrepreneurs vacation in detail by taking a close look at the excuses executives perpetrate for refusing time off. And despite the immediate and long-term benefits of international trips and true time off, CEOs do refuse to take a vacation. We vehemently ignore our accumulated time-off, as if there is an award at the end of our careers for sabotaging personal time.

I soon realized that convincing executives and entrepreneurs to travel required statistics, facts, AND a method for action.

Far too often the business owners and executives that crave experiential, genuine travel don't know where to begin. The task of planning the trip is insurmountable. It's impossible to make it through the planning stages, even when a person understands that vacation is necessary for their mental and physical wellbeing. Or so it seems.

This book provides a guideline and method for taking a vacation, without the stress. I've tailored each piece of advice just for you, the dedicated, driven, work-motived executive. Dive in and stop wondering whether it's possible to take your dream vacation. It is and furthermore planning your vacation can actually be excellent for your business!

You just need to approach time away from the office strategically and thoughtfully. Here's how.

Warmest Regards,
Patrick
Owner of Raiwasa Private Resort & Culture Whisperer

Over the years, vacations became fewer and shorter – some years my only time away from work was on weekends. Other years, I didn't even take weekends.

That all changed in an instant when I sold my business. My family set off on a one-year, around the world trip. Every vacation I didn't take for years and years was bundled into a continuous adventure that made me realize how much my focus on work had cost in terms of mental health, personal relationships, and true happiness.

During this experience, my outlook on life completely changed. At the time I was uncertain, and even pessimistic about this change of perspective, but now it was clearly for the better.

The depth and intensity of this realization requires that I share it with other entrepreneurs, CEOs, and executives! But how could I do this?

Last year I embarked on a project to show executives and entrepreneurs the benefits of experiential travel.

My book *Overworked*: How to Turn Your Vacation into a Competitive Advantage and Bottom Line Profits is a definitive guide to the benefits and of taking a true vacation and demonstrates how taking a vacation ensures you outperform in all areas of your life: Work. Health. Relationships. Financial. Sex. Outlook. Social. Happiness. Job Satisfaction. It's also your go-to place for learning about the mental and emotional upsides of time out of the office.

I've been there too.

I skipped long weekends with my wife and refused holidays with the kids. I sacrificed years of irreplaceable and priceless personal memories to my intense focus at work. And in the moment, it seemed completely worth it!

I reveled in the process of "giving up" a vacation because it showed my commitment to work and total dedication to my company. Also, I loved my job.

I loved my job to the point that everything else could wait. As the owner of a business, my job was also demanding and stressful. On the best days, anxiety was a low hum in the background of a busy office. On many days my work was a high-stress environment that fueled my love of work. I actually craved the stress, and deciding to stay late at the office in the midst of a particularly intense workday was oddly satisfying. My wife, Erika, will tell you that my obsession with work was, in fact, infatuation.

Therefore, I didn't see a skipped vacation as a missed opportunity, but rather, a chance to double-down at the office. My business flourished, which made the inequality in my work-life balance feel justified and necessary.

Then there were the trips I did take.

Travel was always plagued by work calls, mornings spent on email, and full-blown anxiety over what was happening back at the office. My attention to family and loved ones on these trips was equal or less than when I was going into the office.

What's keeping executives tied to the office? It turns out the most significant reasons are related to the planning and pre-vacation process. This widely used excuse is closely followed by a fear of all the office activity that happens while the CEO is away. Here's more detail on why executives don't leave work.

Executives Don't Want to Leave the Office

For a large number of CEOs taking time off work isn't even on the table. These individuals don't give the idea a second thought because they simply don't want to take vacation

Today's business culture commends the workaholic; we reward the people putting the most hours and revere the CEO that has gone five years without a single day off. America respects the workaholic far more than the executive insisting on a healthy work-life balance. An executive can actually find motivation in the results of refusing time away from work.

Without understanding the deep detriment that comes with incessant work, or the profound benefits of travel and vacation, executives and entrepreneurs have blindly bought into a harsh work routine. Ultimately, refusing vacation for reasons of pride, praise or acclaim could hurt a career, relationships, and work performance.

A Deep Fear of Being Replaceable & Replaced

Do you feel irreplaceable at work? If so, you are among the minority of American workers. In polls, the vast majority of people, from CEOs to entry-level employees, express fear of being replaced in the role.

The website Glassdoor, which allows current and former employees to anonymously review their employers, conducts an annual survey on vacation and paid time off. In recent years, this survey not only confirmed the growing trend in the United States of foregoing vacation days but also pinpointed the motivating factors for employees to leave these valuable off days on the table.

The website determined that the majority of Americans rebuffing some or all of their vacation time do so out of the fear that time off will lead to or encourage their replacement. While employees uninvolved in management are more likely to express this sentiment, the same logic is certainly applicable to CEOs and executives.

Even in a company's top positions, there is concern that taking time off will negatively impact performance or influence how the board of directors and ownership view your performance. And while a small drop in performance may not lead to the dismissal of a CEO or other executive, it can negatively impact several other aspects of employment, including annual bonus, salary increase, and trust in the individual's judgment.

Other Executives Feel Irreplaceable – Even for an Hour

Of course, there are many CEOs and entrepreneurs that feel exactly the opposite of replaceable. These are the CEOs among us that believe their role in the business is crucial – so crucial that any amount of time away from work is detrimental. For these executives, refusing vacation is in sacrifice to the company because without their physical presence the business would absolutely suffer.

A similar concern is that no one else at the company could handle a crisis, emergency, or "big" question as effectively as the executive or entrepreneur. To address this fear, preparation, response, and delegation are crucial because it's a founded concern. Likely, there is no one in your organization that can address a concern or solves a problem in the same manner as you would. To maintain maximum decision-making, you need to prepare your team for the possibility that you are unavailable.

However, consider the possibility that by preparing your team for your absence and vacation, you could actually build a stronger organization. Giving your team the tools to address a crisis, take more responsibility, and take new roles leads to substantial improvement even when you are at your desk. We'll talk about this at length in the next chapter.

The Bottom Line: Vacations Stress Us Out

These concerns amass into one motivating factor to stay at the office – stress. CEOs, entrepreneurs, and other employees regularly say that the stress of a vacation simply isn't worth the potential pay off. Instead, they'd rather stay at work and keep grinding. Luckily, a stress-free vacation is possible, and in upcoming chapters, I will give you the tools for making it a reality.

What's even more important, I'll explain why taking a stress-free vacation is the best thing you've done for your business in the last 12 months.

CHAPTER 3

Planning Your Vacation
BENEFITS THE ENTIRE OFFICE

For the most part, executives recognize that taking vacation has mental, emotional, and physical benefits. These are all personal benefits, and all too often that is how all employees, of any level or profession, view vacation – as only a personal positive.

Yet, executive vacation can have substantial benefits across the business! It can be difficult to convince CEOs of this fact, but studies and research have more than proven that properly planning a vacation has seemingly infinite paybacks to the business.

In my first book, *Overworked* I discuss the incredible improvement in productivity that executives experience from a true, experiential vacation. Here, we switch gears and prove that a properly planned, executive vacation actually has productivity benefits across an entire organization.

Dedicating Time to the Parameters of Your Role

Executives, CEOs in particular, spend little time considering the exact parameters of their role. Most people in executive positions have a high-level and overarching job description, but their actual work and big-picture thinking frequently fall far beyond what these written descriptions incorporate.

Just as frequently, what a CEO handles on a daily basis dives into the mundane and detailed, two adjectives that indicate a particular task is better delegated to someone else. But, we'll get to delegation in just a minute.

When an executive starts to plan for travel, it's necessary to consider the bare bones of the position. A CEO or entrepreneur must ask, "What do I handle that no one else in this office can or should do?" Answering this question requires an intense review of daily, weekly, and monthly activities. It requires you to think about what falls outside the individual's job description and most importantly what tasks are wasting time.

Simply going through this process means an executive has a better idea of tasks are creating inefficiencies and causing roadblocks for the company's progress. The impending vacation encourages an executive to work through these issues.

Going on Vacation Requires Delegation

To travel without stress, an executive or entrepreneur has to delegate daily tasks and some decision-making ability to managers, staff, and his or her assistant. It is impossible to take a true, experiential and stress-free vacation without appropriate, proper, and intelligent delegation before you leave the office.

In later chapters, I'll provide exact steps and hints to delegate more effectively, but first I want to prove that delegation is an immediate benefit of taking a vacation. In fact, the benefits of having an effective delegator at the top echelon of business ripple throughout the entire organization. Delegating is characteristic of good executive management and a valued leadership skill.

Four Reasons Delegating Betters a Business

First, delegating frees an executive to focus on the far-reaching and overarching questions that the organization is facing. A CEO or other executive can become bogged down in the day-to-day issues of a business, but this isn't the most effective or highest use of such an individual's time. A CEO is hired to encourage progress, create action, and also have vision. Your vision is certainly short if you don't have the time to move past agendas and calendar invites.

The only way to clear a CEO's schedule is by delegating away time-consuming, detailed, and non-executive tasks. Also, micromanaging a team stifles the business, as I'll talk about next.

Second, delegation allows executives to utilize the strengths of their team. Intelligent delegators notice and absorb the individual talents of their management team and other employees, and then delegate based on these strengths. We'll cover this in more detail, but what's spectacular about delegating based on unique strengths and skills is that it equals higher quality work and more value from employees (without any additional cost).

Third, delegating to your team's strengths also allows those individuals to increase their skill set and expand their knowledge. In other words, an executive that smartly delegates will see that his or her team grows and develops at a far faster pace. The results of this process come full circle when those managers and employees are prepared to take on new responsibilities and bring new perspective to the business. No one is served when an executive stifles employee growth and improvement.

Fourth, a business is better off when employees want to continue their professional growth and constantly take on new work. So, as a final point, delegating highlights the managers and employees hungry for a challenge and to eager to climb the company ladder. Go-getters and company rock stars will be the first employees to accept and conquer new tasks.

Delegating also exposes the employees that are lagging behind or uninspired.

Organizing Your Support Staff

Consistent and well-planned CEO and executive vacation is also a huge boost to administrators and support staff. Of course, these employees benefit when an executive delegates effectively, but there are even greater benefits.

A stress-free vacation requires both the executive and administrative staff to be extremely organized and detailed. Every aspect of the CEO's calendar, email system, means of communication, and core business responsibilities need to be in perfect order before travel. A vast amount of this work falls to administrators.

This intense level of organization invariably cleans up other systems, functions, and processes. The result being all of these administrative tasks are handled more efficiently and effectively.

Wondering what processes to put in place before your vacation You should be - knowing how to effectively utilize your assistant or other support staff is one of the best ways to improve your productivity and take a stress-free vacation. Because it is so important, I'll touch on this topic throughout the book!

CHAPTER 4

Set Your Dates
BEYOND BOOKING A FLIGHT

The question of "when" you take a vacation is arguably the most important one you can ask from a planning perspective.

There is the bigger picture to consider, such as what time of year fits the ebb and flow of your work routine. Then there are the details, for example scheduling an important meeting two weeks, not two days before you leave. Invariably, getting the details right is just as important to a successful, fun, and stress-free vacation.

So, where to begin when planning your next trip? An organized and updated calendar is crucial to your stress-free travel.

Why Do You Always Vacation in July?

The best time for a vacation is when it fits your work schedule. It might seem that I'm starting with common sense here, but historically people didn't plan a vacation based on this itinerary or with this motivation. The origins of the very word vacation are indicative of how time off work was scheduled.

Vacation is derived from the Latin word vacare, which means to be unoccupied. This was adopted into English as the word vacate. Again, with the direct meaning of to leave a place previously occupied. In England, the derived term vacation was used to denote the very specific instance of schoolteachers vacating their classroom for the summer months. It was a specific term for a specific time of year.

Until the mid-19th century, the word vacation was similarly a reference to summer break from classes for the school children and teachers in the United States. However, more of the middle class was experiencing the privilege of a few days or week away from work. For the first time, people could afford to miss their weekly paycheck. Travel became a fashionable way to indicate privilege and financial stability, and with it, broader use of the term vacation.

Here we are approaching 2020, and the majority of Americans and Europeans still plan their vacations in the summer. In fact, half of Americans taking a vacation go during the month of July. Not only does this make July an expensive month to travel, it could make no sense for your work commitments.

I would argue that despite school breaks and annual holidays, weather patterns and high seasons, the best time to "vacation" is when it works for your work schedule. Now, how to set that plan in motion?

Put the Dates on the Calendar

When magazines and researchers ask executives and entrepreneurs why they don't travel, there are inexplicably a handful of responses that all come to a very simply conclusion.

The executives and CEOs line up to say, "I never took a trip because I never set the dates." These are the CEOs that never pull up their work calendar or call their admin to block a week or two off in their schedule.

And putting a vacation on your calendar is more difficult than you think because it's the moment of commitment.

Just as with all other work commitments and projects, the best way to pick the dates of your vacation is through a deadline. Give yourself two weeks to consider the upcoming 10 or 12 months of work. Think about what meetings are crucial and the major project schedules throughout the year. Are you overhauling a key product or moving offices? Does your office have a busy season? When are your clients the most busy or suppliers the most unreliable? Take the time to consider these questions and concerns, and then put the dates on the calendar.

Most importantly, the earlier you can pick your dates and announce them to the management team, the better. Also, it's extremely helpful to have your admin and support staff looped in on vacation dates early on. Then your staff can also alleviate schedule conflicts and maneuver important deadlines.

Respect Your Trip Dates

Looking for a stress-free vacation? You can't simply decide on two weeks to take off and then forget about it until the day before. A successful vacation required intelligent scheduling decisions in the months before you leave.

Yet, respecting your vacation schedule is far more time consuming and complicated than putting it on your calendar. Work will constantly try to impede the dates you chose - no matter how well reasoned your dates were months before.

As a rule, I try to have all major meetings and deadlines handled two weeks before international travel. Rarely will I allow staff to schedule key meetings for the week I return from vacation, and if a major deadline requires my approval or oversight, then it shouldn't be in my first week back.

Of course, there are always complications. Whether a supplier is pushing for a specific date or a commercial contract is closing within a set timeframe, you will encounter unavoidable deadlines. The best way to handle these issues isn't with defeat and trip cancellation, but by reaffirming in meetings and calls that you are away those days and handling the deadline or closing will be delegated.

The Two-Day Rule of All Travel

With all the hurdles and possible roadblocks, how does any CEO make it from dates on a calendar to the airplane? One trick is when blocking out their work schedule and making vacation announcements to staff, they pad the front and back end of their tip with extra days. Typically, these executives say they are out of the office one day before they actually leave and are set to return one day after they really land.

This "two-day rule" gives you an extra day to handle last minute details and emergencies at the office, without interrupting your true trip schedule. And when you return a day early you can make the decision to work from home or head into the office early.

CHAPTER 5

Your Mindset About Travel
DOES MATTER

It is now two months before you leave on vacation. Likely, you haven't hit extensive anxiety, but your trip is probably in the back of your mind. As you decide on follow up and action items from meetings, you are now thinking about how that work will impact your time away or vice versa.

The thoughts of many CEOs: my vacation is going to become a problem for progress and productivity at work.

If you want to stay stress-free during the time leading up to your vacation, you must change your mindset about travel. For many executives and entrepreneurs, time away from the office is as much an impediment, as it is a privilege. While you know it's intended to be an enjoyable experience, there is probably a small part of you that wonders if walking away is really going to make you any happier or any more productive.

First of all, the answer is yes. Time off is overwhelmingly shown to increase a CEO's productivity and decision-making capability back at the office. Travel is also closely linked to joy, happiness, and contentment, even after a trip has ended. CEOs and executives that take a true vacation are better leaders and better people. Which means, second, it is absolutely time that you adjust your mindset about travel.

The Mindset You Probably Have Before a Trip

The travel conglomerate Wyndham Vacation Rentals found that 37% of all Americans cancel their vacation after it's already planned and booked. Even if there isn't a refund or repayment waiting, CEOs are very likely to back out of vacation plans. The reason for this lack of follow through is, for the most part, a bad mindset about taking the trip.

People anticipate that their vacation will be stressful and complicated. We assume that the issues in planning our vacation will outweigh the benefits. In reality, it's this approach to travel that makes those downsides a reality. If you feel handcuffed to your company, then you will be.

The Mindset You Need Before a Trip

Start by thinking of vacation as a business benefit. And I don't mean in the same sense as healthcare or company car. A CEO taking time to travel isn't just a personal benefit or incentive for accepting a job.

Employee vacation generally is a benefit to the business, no matter where you stand on the corporate ladder. It's easier to walk away when you trip provides more than personal gain. And it's true that the implications of your vacation are a boost to the business.

Your approach to vacation is a tagline. You should use it often, put it on a Post-It, tell it to your spouse, and believe it – even as a major sales contract comes through a month before you leave.

How Your Mindset Can Improve Office Culture & Productivity

Company culture about vacation is set from the top down. If the executives of a company are pessimistic about time away from the office, so will upper management. This same mindset trickles down to managers and mid-level employees. If you forgo travel and worship overworking, so will your employees

At first glance, employees willing to give up their vacation might seem a good thing for productivity, but it isn't. These employees are far less likely to stay with the company, be happy in the office, and produce exceptional work product. Eventually, the top-notch employees in your business will leave for a healthier work environment.

The lesson here is that your mindset about vacation matters for the entire company, not just your annual trip.

CHAPTER 6

Talk About Your Trip,
WITH EVERYONE

If you are looking for a simple way to improve your vacation experience, you should begin by talking about the trip! Keeping travel a secret at the office isn't going to benefit anyone. In fact, a covert vacation is a huge detriment to the enjoyment of your trip and productivity of your team back at the office.

Employees, management and other executives need to know about your vacation. And if you are serious about stress-free travel, then you want them to know early in the process!

Problems When Your Vacation Is a Secret

Bad habits are difficult to break. For many executives, it's actually a tough challenge to talk openly about their vacation plans. Even revealing the dates of a trip is difficult for some executives. Very few high-powered personnel give away the specifics of their destination and travel plans.

We've developed the bad habit of believing vacation is better when work isn't aware of our absence. To this end, most CEOs try to slip out of the office unnoticed, except by a small circle of support staff. There are clear problems when an executive doesn't tell his or her entire team about a vacation. For starters, it is nearly impossible for a CEO to be away for a week or two weeks without rousing the suspicion and rumor mill of the office.

Then there are a slew of more practical problems. Let's discuss them briefly.

Problem 1: You Can't Delegate

First, if you don't inform the office of your vacation, you can't delegate. In the next chapter, I'll cover delegation in-depth, so suffice it to say that without delegating a true vacation is impossible.

Problem 2: Emergencies Become Big Business Issues

If your team is unaware of your absence, learning about it during an emergency increases the anxiety of the situation. If there is a decision or question that truly needs your immediate attention, and an employee only learns you are unreachable in the midst of the situation, chances are it will take longer to solve and come to a less satisfactory conclusion.

Prior communication about your trip, including destination, emergency contact information, and expected response time helps your team make smart decisions, even if temporary decisions, if something happens during your vacation.

Problem 3: You Are More Likely to Cancel Your Vacation

There will always be a complication with a contract, a personnel problem, or supplier issue. If you haven't told anyone about your vacation, then these problems make great excuses to cancel your vacation. If this doesn't sound like a problem, then you should pick up a copy of my other book *Overworked*.

In *Overworked* I discuss the benefits of vacation, and why America's deep aversion to vacation is problematic for both the individual and business.

Problem 4: The Company Will Lose Productivity and Momentum

Finally, keeping your vacation a secret prevents upper management from supporting your trip.

If another vice president or manager doesn't know you've left for vacation, it's impossible for them to alleviate the complications in your work schedule or take on extra tasks. These essential employees can't mitigate an emergency and they don't know to direct emails to a different individual.

Instead, you'll receive an onslaught of questions and emails that require an immediate response. Even with an out of office response turned on, the barrage of emails and somewhat important communication can quickly ruin your vacation.

Informing key members of the organization about your vacation allows the entire company to operate more effectively in your absence. Basically, it's good for business when employees know you are away, which is the main reason you should tell everyone about your incredible trip.

Shut Down the Shame of Vacation

The main reason most executives choose to keep quiet about vacation is the implication they shouldn't be taking one. CEOs and entrepreneurs want to be seen as completely and entirely dedicated to their career. As I discussed in my introduction, it's a compliment to be a workaholic, and going on a true vacation shatters this image.

Alternatively, if you think about vacation as necessary and instrumental in the longevity of your career and pertinent to the success of the business, it becomes far easier to share your plans. As a high level, influential part of the business, it's your responsibility to shut down the shame of taking a vacation and highlight the substantial benefits that come from travel.

Here's Your Plan

When you put your vacation on the calendar, share it with your admin and other support staff.

Three months before your trip, send an email informing the entire team of your intended vacation. Before this you should let key members of your team know, such as individuals that may need to assume additional responsibilities or team members that should schedule deadlines around your trip.

One month before your trip follow up with other executives and managers about the timing and any complications. This is also a good time to start discussions of delegating specific task and projects to other people, and a poignant time for checking with your support staff that the dates are still clear of major work conflicts. A month before still gives you opportunity to work around these conflicts, reschedule major issues, and travel stress-free.

Two weeks before your trip, your upcoming travels should be common knowledge and part of regular discussions. You want to confirm with managers that there aren't any serious concerns or issues to handle before you leave and start to dig into other final plans.

CHAPTER 7

At All Times
DELEGATE TO YOUR ASSISTANT

The Important Role of an Executive Assistant

There's a good reason your executive assistant is often described as a gatekeeper. A great assistant is the driving force behind your daily agenda, weekly schedule, and ultimately what issues receive your attention. He or she also holds significant power to influence which employees schedule time on your calendar and make it into your office. While there are hundreds of business decisions that could land on your desk each day, each is first filtered through your support staff.

For most executives, his or her assistant is the dictator of what receives consideration Monday morning, and what's pushed to Friday at 4:00 PM.

If you want to be successful as an executive, you need an exceptional person to fill the role of your executive assistant. Here's why. Your assistant influences not only focus and workload, but is also the gatekeeper of your overall organization - handling schedules, deadlines, and agendas. With an ultra-talented executive assistant on your team, your day runs smoother and distractions are limited.

Literally, your assistant can determine if a day is productive or a total waste.

What Should Your Executive Assistant Do?

Some CEOs are fantastic at sending work to an executive assistant, but most of us could use serious practice. Statistics say that the majority of executives are risk takers, but enjoy a high degree of control. By nature, this makes all of us in the C Suite bad delegators, despite the obvious need for directing other people. Curious what most executives have their assistants handle, whether they have impending travel or not?

Most people assign their calendar, including the creation of meeting invites and blocking off personal appointments to their assistants. As part of this process, an executive assistant should also handle preparing documents and agendas for any meetings, and send revisions to invites, if a change occurs.

An executive assistant is in the best position to handle the organization of your physical space. This includes straightening your office, sorting printed papers, and keeping your desk uncluttered. Part of this responsibility is policing who comes into your office and when. While you are away on vacation this role may seem less important, but it's actually imperative. An executive assistant can rearrange furniture or files that aren't streamlined or effective and literally improve your office while you aren't in it.

Your assistant should be instrumental in planning and carry out all of your business travel. An ideal system involves you giving basic instructions, such as "I like to leave on Monday mornings and return on Thursdays before noon," the name of your preferred airline, and preferences on hotel features, and car rentals. Then, just augmenting these preferences with specific instructions before each trip.

Hopefully, your assistant is already handling most travel plans; so what else can support staff handle to make you more productive at work?

Four Tasks Your Assistant Should Handle, But Probably Isn't

One: your assistant should have regularly screen what's in your inbox.

This means sorting every email into a specified folder based on content and providing low-level responses.

Two: your assistant should control a master list of your projects and responsibilities.

The details of this list are specific to a CEO, for example, how much information you want on this master list. But having an overview of each and every requirement can truly help with meeting deadlines and understanding roadblocks. The outcome is your assistant can control your personal task list the way a project manager conducts multiple people in the business.

Three: make your assistant responsible for tech problems.

While skills in Word, Excel, and tools such as CMS are imperative, your assistant doesn't need to handle the details of a tech issue, just create the plan of action for solving the problem. For instance, if a projector stops working or a PowerPoint won't load, your assistant is the go-between in contacting an IT expert and having the equipment returned to working order.

Four: put your assistant in charge of employee complaints and personnel problems.

Again, this doesn't mean support staff is the arbitrator over interoffice disputes, but he or she is responsible for orchestrating the outcome. Whether your assistant takes the matter to human resources or provides you with a brief overview of the issue, interoffice problems shouldn't be a distraction on your desk.

What Else Can You Delegate?

You are probably thinking that there is other work that can't be delegated to your assistant, such as, projects and substantive tasks that need to be handed off to managers and department heads.
Never fear, I'll cover the upside of delegating down the pipeline in the next chapter.

CHAPTER 8

The Details of Delegating
BEFORE YOU TRAVEL

Logically, you already know that business doesn't stop just because you leave the office. Yet, many executives irrationally fear that this is exactly what will happen when they walk away. There is real concern that in the week, two weeks, or month they are away the company will come to a standstill. Dare I say there is fear that an executive vacation could kill the company?

While you logically know the company isn't going to shut down without your physical presence in the office, a reduction in productivity is very possible. Concern for decisions, deals, and overall work product from the office is a legitimate and intelligent concern.

How can you avoid delays and decreased productivity during a vacation? Easy, just delegate.

Of course, delegating your daily work is more complex in practice. To begin, an executive needs to be a skilled delegator before vacation is even on the horizon. So, that's where I'll begin. With the reasons and tips for delegating, no matter how far off your travel date is.

Delegating Gives You a Better Return on Investment

Let's think of your managers and employees as resources. In actuality, your team is the most important resource in your business, but we rarely talk about delegating in these terms.

If your employees are a resource, then you want to receive the highest possible return on investment (ROI) from these employees as possible. You want the greatest possible work product, in the fastest time, for the least amount of money. Delegating maximizes your ROI.

Through delegation, you are allowing your lowest paid and least knowledgeable employees handle the most legwork. Meanwhile, you are giving these employees the responsibility and know-how to advance their career and achieve a promotion. At the same time your own salary isn't wasted on menial tasks and time-consuming projects. Across the board, this maximizes the money spent on payroll.

The single best way to increase the company's ROI is continuously to ask, "Can someone else handle this task?"

Avoid the Last Minute Scramble

Delegating is truly about planning ahead, and as you've probably realized a stress-free vacation is built on extensive prior planning. If you want to delegate part of a project or divvy up the entire thing among different employees, you need to organize the process.

Delegating requires an executive or entrepreneur to outline the goals of a project, assign the pieces to managers and team members, and decide which employees are best equipped to take what work. And delegating works best when this process occurs well before a deadline.

Employees are going to respond best to take on new tasks when they have plenty of time to complete the work and they are given clear reasons why they were selected for the project.

Pushing Work Down the Pipeline Builds Your Team

Need another reason to invest in effective delegating? Delegating allows you to simultaneously learn more about your employees and build their skills. You'll quickly realize which employees are capable of taking on additional work and accomplishing higher-level projects. That builds confidence in giving these employees more responsibility. And you'll equip them with new knowledge and experience to advance their development further and faster.

Tips to Delegate More Effectively Before Your Trip

In the months before you go on vacation, you can make yourself entirely replaceable for a week or two, simply by delegating. What should you know to delegate yourself straight out of the office?

Delegate based on obvious and already developed strengths. In the weeks or month before your trip is not the time to try and train or guide an employee. What you need is someone already capable of the work and poised to take on a new responsibility. This works best when you delegate on the basis of known strengths.

For example, if you need someone to handle responses to a difficult client while you are away, look for a talented communicator. Perhaps you need someone comfortable with conflict, but levelheaded and even-tempered. The difficulty in this style of delegation is knowing your employees well enough to assign tasks and responsibility in this manner. Here, CEOs and other executives can often rely on their managers for insight or delegating down the line.

Another tip for delegating just before your trip is certain to give clear guidelines and direction. Very likely the manager receiving instruction doesn't have complete knowledge of the project. You are probably asking an employee to take on responsibility without knowing the full scope of the project. The person needs clear instructions on deadlines, format, other time factors, and providing progress reports.

Finally, in the weeks before you leave, be certain to provide feedback on any responsibilities you've previously delegated. Check-in with the managers that have undertaken new tasks in earlier weeks and try to prevent any major complications arising while you are away.

CHAPTER 9

The Two Weeks
BEFORE YOU LEAVE

Two weeks before your trip is a crucial moment if you want time away from the office to be successful. This timeframe is close enough to your vacation that the big-ticket items, like flights and accommodation, are handled, and you can focus on the details at work. But two weeks is also far enough away from your travel date to meet any problems head on.

I've developed a list of six things you should do two weeks before you leave for a true vacation.

#1: Create & Disseminate an Emergency Process

You are going to be away from the office. You may not be immediately reachable by phone or email - I'd advocate that the harder you are to contact, the better. But you still need an emergency plan. Two weeks before you leave for vacation, you should create this plan and share it with your admin or executive assistant.

In this plan should be straightforward steps for reaching you while away, including contact information and the names and contact information of manager to contact if you can't be reached. Make this a step-by-step process, and during hand-off give clear examples of emergency circumstances. When should your admin simply send an email? What reasons justify a phone call? When should the hotel be contacted and what information should be relayed?

The more instruction you can provide in this emergency plan, the better.

#2: Confirm Your Going Away Game Plan

Another important conversation with your assistant is covering all non-emergency processes. You should clarify what will happen with your emails, what phone calls should be answered, and what information to provide clients or suppliers. There should be a process and plan for all tasks that typically cross your desk, and two weeks before you should confirm that everything is covered and considered.

#3: List Your Work in Order of Priority

Your team is capable of running the office for a week or two without you. What your employees can't do is read your mind. Therefore, the more details and instruction you can provide the better. A great resource for managers is a list of tasks and projects in order of priority. This helps key employees to see the workload through your eyes and approach tasks and time management as you would.

This extra guidance can go a long way towards avoiding disappointment and frustration when you return.

#4: Arrange for Your Admin to Create a Daily Report

A small number of CEOs will entirely walk away from the office for a week or two. Then there are the rest of us – incapable of completely letting go. Yet, an intention to check your email once a day can quickly evolve into hours on your laptop, which isn't a healthy way to spend your trip. Instead of going through your Inbox every morning of vacation, leave that to your assistant. He or she can sort the bulk of the information, delegate tasks to capable managers, and provide you an overview of the information. That leaves you with one email to draft, a single response back to your admin with instructions on outstanding issues.

#5: Sit Down with Your "Second in Command"

I've found that your assistant is the best resource while you are out of the office. Support staff is best positioned to ensure you are organized, informed, handle small "fires", and prepared for your return. Yet, you admin probably isn't going to handle substantive work while you are away. This is where delegating comes into play.

As you assign the core of your daily duties to different team members, you need a manager or other executive to whom these employees can report. This is your second in command and an important part of your stress-free vacation strategy.

Two weeks before your vacation sit down for a cup of coffee or lunch with this executive or manager. Discuss the chain of communication, responsibilities you've delegated to other employees, and brief them on potential roadblocks or complexities.

#6: Inform High Priority People Outside Your Office

While preparing your internal team for your out time out the office is most important, there are probably external clients and contacts that need to know about your upcoming absence. Unless there are special circumstances, two weeks is typically enough time for these people to plan your vacation.

As with any rule, there are some exceptions, if a major deadline falls during your holiday, you probably want to communicate with affected individuals a month or two before your trip.

CHAPTER 10

What to Do
TWO DAYS BEFORE YOU FLY

Here's the thing, an international trip, particularly one where you intend to sign off and disconnect from the office (which you should), can be extremely hectic on the day before you leave. The phenomenon of serious stress 24 hours before a flight has encouraged many CEOs and executives to do things differently. And if you haven't copied their example, it's time you do!

The strategy: tell everyone you are leaving work a day earlier than your flight itinerary. This gives you an extra day (or two) to decompress at home and truly put yourself in the mood for a vacation. It also gives you some extra time, without the office interruptions and distracting co-worker conversations, to handle any last minute business.

With this plan in mind, most of your final preparations at the office should happen two days before you fly.

Some Details You Can't Overlook

In many ways, CEOs and other executives are required to be big picture people. Even while talking about the nitty-gritty details of a project or employee issue, you must keep the broader impact on the organization in mind. But whether you are a detail-oriented person or detest getting down in the weeds of an issue, a successful vacation, in many ways, depends on you carrying about them.

There are a number of small things you can do at the office to ensure a better vacation. For example, prepare a list of usernames and passwords for your admin to access in an emergency. This list should include the necessary information to access your computer. While we store a great deal of data on our devices, such as mobile phones and laptops, you probably have documents, reports, and other information only found on your computer. There are several tools out there that can help you organize, track, and protect your passwords. For example I use a program called 1Password. This tool allows you to securely store your passwords and give specific access to your assistant (http://www.agilebits.com).

Another detailed task is cleaning out your inbox. If you took the advice to delegate appropriately, support staff should already be sorting and organizing your inbox, but there are likely many unimportant or unnecessary messages that made it past this first line of defense. Before you leave on your trip, it's important to purge your inbox of anything unnecessary and create tasks for those messages that need a response.

You could be wondering why is cleaning out your inbox so important?

First, while you are away a clean inbox will help you find information quickly, and spend less time sorting through old messages to find one piece of information. Also, when you return, you'll start with a clean slate and fewer distractions.

But Leave Most Organizational Tasks to Your Assistant

While handling certain organizational details is unavoidable, CEOs are smarter to leave the bulk of the minute tasks to an assistant. For example, you don't need to spend your last few hours in the office setting an out of office message.

The time to assign these responsibilities is in the days and weeks before your trip as they come to mind. However, you should cover each one last time with your assistant before leaving.

What tasks are we talking about here?

To start, have your assistant take care of your out of office email. This includes drafting it, setting it, and sending an initial response to highly important incoming messages. Your assistant can also set and schedule your out of office voicemail and organize the stream of messages you receive when you are away. The same system can work for any interoffice chats or project management systems.

While you are traveling is also a good time for your assistant to rearrange and unclutter the physical space. I touched on this earlier, but your time away from the office can be used in a manner to make you highly productive and far more efficient upon your return. Better organization is the key to all of this.

Organizing your office, cleaning your desk, and sorting any physical files, contracts, or papers are perfect responsibilities for while you're gone. An organized space can immediately improve your mood and productivity after a vacation.

Lastly, each job will have organizational requirements that would build up or become chaotic in your absence. It could be the process of approving expense reports requires your signature or you instruct IT to run specific system updates. Give someone in your office the authority and instructions to handle these reoccurring processes, rather than leaving them for your return.

The One Thing You Can't Delegate

Two days before your trip there should be an air of excitement and anticipation. But for many CEOs, the days preceding a trip are anything but exciting. Instead, high power executives often spend these days waffling between backing out and cutting the trip short.

In these two days before a trip, you have to embrace the experience. A stress-free trip isn't built on delegating and details alone but requires the right mindset. In fact, as I discussed in earlier chapters, your mindset about a vacation is probably the most determinative factor to the actual experience.

CHAPTER 11

Benefits of Truly Walking AWAY FROM WORK

You've booked flights, packed bags, prepared everyone at work, had your assistant set an out of office response and now it's time to take the final step towards a stress-free vacation. It's time to turn off your notifications and put your phone into airplane mode.

Admittedly, there are very few CEOs and executives that could leave their mobile phones at home during travel. Even if all you'll access during your trip is intermittent Wi-Fi, there's a high probability that your mobile phone is making the cut of important items to pack.

However, each one of us is capable of putting rules in place regarding devices and office communication. Clear boundaries about when and how you are going to answer work messages and what counts as an emergency help you have a more rewarding vacation and reap more benefits from the experience.

So, what do you gain by truly walking away from work?

Better Culture Around Vacation Back at the Office

I'll touch on the personal benefits of a true vacation, such as increased happiness and improved mental outlook, but also many positives of your decreased connectivity are playing out back at the office.

If you disconnect or set reasonable boundaries on your vacation communication, other employees will do the same. Your ability to truly walk away indicates that vacation is expected, healthy, and important. That means more employees will emulate your example, and they will also prioritize taking an experiential and beneficial vacation.

Just as a vacation has substantial personal benefits to CEOs and executives, the same is true for all other employees. So, if your employees are going on vacation they are also likely to be happier and more productive back at work. Ultimately, this is going to improve the culture and atmosphere in your office. And to think, you're company reaps all of these rewards simply because executives are able to put down their cell phones.

More Responsible and Independent Team

If you micromanage from a distance by checking in 15 different times a day and suffocating employees, even while in Fiji, your team doesn't internalize the significant benefits of delegation and new responsibilities. In other words, as you spend yet another vacation in front of your laptop, your team is remaining totally and completely stagnant back at the office. This serves no one.

Alternatively, you could be enjoying quality, stress-free time with your family and the individuals you left in charge during a true vacation could have an opportunity for immense professional growth.

A big benefit for your office is that with you away on a true vacation, your team is required to handle minor issues and everyday decisions. Certain employees will rise to the occasion and start to take on management roles or responsibilities. Other employees will learn the requirements of a new task or job. In both of these cases, you'll return to a much more capable and proficient office than the one you left.

Your Return to the Office Will Be Better

Not only are you guaranteed to have experience less stress during travel if you unplug and create some distance (literally and figuratively) from the office, you're also going to have a better first day back. A great quote in the world of vacation research and tourism today is that you need to disconnect to reconnect, and it's true.

As an executive, you need time away. It's necessary for the longevity of your career and improves most aspects of your work performance. But if you refuse to set down your phone or turn off the laptop, you'll return of the office in the same fragmented, exhausted condition that you left – even if you don't immediately realize it.

Just as you took steps to set yourself up for a stress-free vacation, you need to give yourself the opportunity for a true vacation. This is how you make a stress-free vacation outlast the dates you are away from the office.

CHAPTER 12

Your Triumphant Return to Work:
HOW TO STAY STRESS-FREE

Have you ever returned from travel feeling refreshed and inspired, only to walk into the office and immediately feel the benefits of holiday slip away? Within a week, you are back to your routine, which is a positive for your personal life and job, but you are unable to obtain any long-term improvements from your trip. The lack of substantial, lasting benefits is a huge negative.

Most people travel the entire arc of their career in this unfortunate pattern of vacation preparation, rejuvenating experience, and quick return to their prior existence. However, this isn't the only option. You can actually return to work triumphantly and maintain the effects of a stress-free vacation for weeks and months to come.

Fly Under the Radar for a Few Days

There is a literal sense of escape that you get on vacation that simply can't be replicated in the office. Yet, you can give yourself a few free minutes in the day to relive the travel experience and recreate the relaxation of travel, simply by keeping your return to the office a quiet one.

There's no need to broadcast your presence back at the office. Your assistant will clearly see you walk in the door and most managers are unlikely to forget the date of your return. Other people throughout the office can learn that you are back through the office gossip mill, which gives you a few days to settle in and catch up on key projects.

Another benefit of keeping your return to the office quiet, you can observe and gain insight into how the office operated while you were away. Consider if a manager is able to consistently handle additional tasks or if a specific process is better delegated away on a permanent basis.

Review Tasks and Projects by Priority, Not Chronology

A great role for your executive assistant is organizing information for your return. On your first day back, tell your assistant that you want a task and project list already prepared. This list should be based on missed emails and phone calls and organized in terms of priority, not receipt or chronology. As you sit down at your desk, don't tackle your inbox or voicemails in chronological order either; rather, go through them based on the priority list provided by your support staff.

This will help you see any major problems or issues in need of attention. If you tackle these pressing issues upfront, you won't have the added stress of discovering a task when it's too late or overdue.

A physical list can also help you stay on task as you catch up. After a vacation it can feel like a CEO or executive is pulled in a million different directions, and so for a week or more nothing is actually accomplished. Instead, stay on your list and don't allow outside distractions until everything necessary is checked off.

Put Yourself on the Clock

There is a very real pressure and incentive to overwork your first week or two back from vacation. With a list of outstanding items and not enough hours in the day to complete them, you may find yourself staying until all hours of the day and night in an effort to catch up. Nothing dispels that feel-good, refreshed-from-vacation feeling faster than a few sleepless nights and mind-numbing days.

Understandably there are a few things that you must accomplish on day one back at the office. The same is true of day two, day three, and every day that follows after a vacation, So, instead of trying to claw your way back to an average day in the initial 48-hours you are back at work, set a deadline for leaving the office – and stick to it.

Maintain a Few Vacation Indulgences

We tend to go easier on ourselves while on vacation. It's perfectly fine to eat the extra cookie. There's nothing wrong with hitting the snooze twice or even three times. No pressure to wear the uncomfortable shoes or put on the uncomfortable suit jacket. Keeping a few of these indulgences in the days and weeks after you return to work can also help maintain the vacation mindset.

Whether you have a chocolate purchased on your trip each night or opt for a glass or red wine those first evenings, it's actually beneficial to allow yourself a few treats. And as the vacation mindset and rejuvenation do start to fade - know that it isn't time to mourn the loss of these benefits, but simply time to calendar your next trip.

CHAPTER 13

Are You Ready for a Vacation?
TRY OUR SCORECARD!

Here is a unique tool to determine if you are ready to take a vacation. This short, yet highly effective, scorecard helps you determine if both your mindset and planning are aligned with the goals of a stress-free vacation.

There are six questions below, each question asks you to consider where you are on a scale of 1 to 12 when it comes to preparing for an upcoming vacation. Before you answer any of these questions, think about how many points out of the total 84, you need to feel entirely prepared to leave for your trip.

Set this number as your target, and something to reach for if you don't have enough points from your first time completing the scorecard.

Question #1:
Did You Commit to Your Vacation When You Booked the Flight?

Where You Are		Where You Want to Be
1	You never put your trip on the calendar or informed the office because you were always going to cancel the day before.	1
2		2
3		3
4	After booking your flight, the trip never crossed your mind again – until the week you are meant to leave.	4
5		5
6		6
7	About a month before your trip you mentioned the possibility to your support staff and have those days showing as "private"– just in case.	7
8		8
9		9
10	You decided on dates and blocked off the time on your work schedule four months or more before your vacation	10
11		11
12		12

Question #2:
Are You Informing Support Staff and Direct Reports in Advance?

Where You Are		Where You Want to Be
1	You're on the plane and no one at the office is certain if this is the first day of your vacation, or if you are even taking one.	1
2		2
3		3
4	You gave your assistant a heads up about the trip about a week ago. You may mention it again as you leave the office the day before.	4
5		5
6		6
7	You shared your calendar event – including emergency contact info- with the admins and managers in the office a month before your vacation.	7
8		8
9		9
10	You sent a detailed email to support staff and managers a month before your trip and subsequently met with certain people about their responsibilities.	10
11		11
12		12

Question #3:
Do You Have the Right Mindset About Vacation?

Where You Are		Where You Want to Be
1	What does it matter? You're more likely to cancel the flight than get on it anyway	1
2		2
3		3
4	Vacation could be a good idea; provided, a million things don't go wrong and your spouse booked the perfect accommodation.	4
5		5
6		6
7	After everything at work is organized you know that taking a few days away is not only beneficial but necessary to your career.	7
8		8
9		9
10	Yes!	10
11		11
12		12

Question #4:
Are You Effectively Delegating Before Your Trip?

Where You Are		Where You Want to Be
1	Even though you're in Fiji, you expect your day-to-day routine will be the exact same, including work responsibilities.	1
2		2
3		3
4	You mentioned to your assistant on a Tuesday that it would be nice if, "things were more organized" when you returned to the office.	4
5		5
6		6
7	You drafted an email dictating the expectations while you were away and assigning a replacement person for all necessary tasks.	7
8		8
9		9
10	You made a list of all tasks that needed delegating, assigned them by email, and followed up with in-person meetings to confirm everything was covered.	10
11		11
12		12

Question #5:
Do You Have a Plan for Two Weeks Before You Leave?

Where You Are		Where You Want to Be
1	That seems like an unnecessary thing to consider. Don't people just "leave" for vacation?	1
2		2
3		3
4	If by a plan, you actually mean make a packing list at your desk? Then, yes.	4
5		5
6		6
7	You've scheduled some time with your assistant and will probably run into enough managers in the hall to pass things off.	7
8		8
9		9
10	Calendar invites for conversations with key employees are sent and you'll have all deadlines and projects completed before the two-week date.	10
11		11
12		12

Question #6:
Have You Thought of the Details to Handle Two Days Before Your Trip?

Where You Are		Where You Want to Be
1	Of course, your flight is at 10:00 am, so you need to arrive at the airport by 8:00 am. Oh, back at the office? Honestly, no. You're simply trying to tick off the big ticket items like the contract deadline that falls on the day you leave. You've set aside a buffer day to clean off your desk and purchase a new bathing suit. You'll also draft the ideal out of office response. Yes, you've handed off most of the details and organizational tasks to your assistant to complete and put time on your calendar for the others.	1
2		2
3		3
4		4
5		5
6		6
7		7
8		8
9		9
10		10
11		11
12		12

Question #7:
What's Your Plan for Returning to the Office?

Where You Are		Where You Want to Be
1	If you never leave, you never have to plan for coming back.	1
2		2
3		3
4	Stay in a consistent caffeine high until your task list is entirely checked off.	4
5		5
6		6
7	Maintain the vacation mindset by practicing the meditative breathing you learned in Fiji and hanging up a souvenir in your office.	7
8		8
9		9
10	Keep your return quiet for the first week, set timeframes for the hours you work each day, prioritize work by immediacy, not chronology, and avoid distractions.	10
11		11
12		12

CHAPTER 14

WHERE TO TAKE YOUR GETAWAY

It's Time to Start Planning

No matter how ready you feel for a vacation or the results of your Scorecard in Chapter 13 (haven't taken it? time to backtrack!), it's probably time to start planning for travel.

Ask yourself these questions. Have you taken a vacation this year? Do you have one planned in for the next six months? Did you take one last year? Have you taken a single day off this decade?

If these seem like reasonable, rational questions to ask, but the answer is no - then it is undoubtedly time for you to plan a vacation.

For the sake of your work productivity, family relationships, and overall happiness, you need to travel, experience and live outside the office. If you don't take the opportunity to vacation and enjoy other aspects of life, you are limiting the possibilities of your perspective and interests. Not to mention tying your existence exclusively to the concept of work and work success.

However, one thing we haven't really discussed amidst all the tips on planning and preparation back at the office is whether where you go on vacation matters. It does!

Location, Location, Location

CEOs and other executives need to choose a vacation destination and accommodation that suits their specific wants and needs. When you start to take a hard look at where to book your trip, you'll find that most places don't meet these qualifications. But there is a place, on the incredible island of Taveuni in Fiji that does.

Raiwasa Private Resort isn't just a vacation destination or another dot on the map. This boutique property provides the height of exclusivity and luxury, all with the CEO approach in mind. How does Raiwasa achieve meet the expectations of CEOs? It is designed and owned by one.

As a former CEO and workaholic, I understand what you're looking for in a vacation – and also some of the details that make a trip easier for CEOs. To ensure you choose a vacation conducive to the CEO mindset and lifestyle, I invite you to stay at a special place in Fiji, Raiwasa Private Resort, WINNER OF THE COVETED WORLD BOUTIQUE HOTEL AWARDS FOR AUSTRALASIA.

As one of Fiji's premier, boutique properties Raiwasa is a lavish and indulgent experience. Yet, it is so much more! Our dedication to experiential travel and total privacy is unique in the Fijian market, and our team can't wait to help you vacation, entirely stress-free.

To finally take the stress-free trip you deserve, call our booking office in the United States at +1-310-598-2176. You can also always find more information about Raiwasa online at *www.fijiluxuryvacation.com* or *www.raiwasa.com.*

Are you ready?
Just contact me.

A PLACE TO TRULY RELAX

RECONNECT WITH YOUR LOVED ONES.
BE GRATEFUL FOR WHAT YOU HAVE.
INDULGE IN HUMAN PLEASURES.
BE IN THE MOMENT.

WITH HAPPINESS ALL AROUND™

www.raiwasa.com
info@raiwasa.com   Tel: +1-310-598-2176

SOURCES:

CHAPTER 2
1. https://www.marketwatch.com/story/55-of-american-workers-dont-take-all-their-paid-vacation-2016-06-15
2. https://www.theguardian.com/money/2015/sep/07/america-vacation-workaholic-culture-labor-day
3. https://www.forbes.com/sites/kateashford/2017/05/31/vacation/#3fc3d6bb726a
4. https://www.projecttimeoff.com/research/state-american-vacation-2016
5. https://www.cnbc.com/2016/12/20/3-reasons-why-half-of-american-workers-are-not-using-their-vacation.html
6. https://www.inc.com/jessica-stillman/case-against-taking-a-vacation.html
7. http://edition.cnn.com/2011/TRAVEL/05/23/vacation.in.america/index.html

CHAPTER 3
1. https://www.totaljobs.com/careers-advice/job-profile/executive-jobs/ceo-job-description
2. https://www.inc.com/david-finkel/10-tips-to-leverage-your-personal-assistant-to-get-more-done-in-less-time.html
3. https://clearconceptinc.ca/how-to-leverage-your-assistant-effectively/
4. http://workawesome.com/productivity/how-to-best-utilize-your-personal-assistant/
5. https://www.hrpayrollsystems.net/why-vacations-are-good-for-business/
6. https://hbr.org/2016/07/the-data-driven-case-for-vacation
7. https://managementstudyguide.com/importance_of_delegation.htm
8. http://www.telegraph.co.uk/connect/better-business/leadership/how-to-delegate-and-why-its-important/
9. https://www.entrepreneur.com/article/279141
10. https://hbr.org/2012/07/why-arent-you-delegating

CHAPTER 4
1. http://www.businessinsider.com/8-things-to-do-at-work-before-your-next-vacation-2014-4?IR=T
2. http://www.smead.com/Director.aspx?NodeId=1740
3. https://www.npr.org/templates/story/story.php?storyId=105545388
4. http://news.gallup.com/poll/6112/majority-americans-plan-vacation-summer.aspx
5. http://theeverygirl.com/how-to-plan-your-work-schedule-for-a-true-vacation/
6. https://www.theglobeandmail.com/report-on-business/careers/career-advice/life-at-work/why-you-should-use-your-work-time-to-plan-your-next-holiday/article34487802/
7. https://www.travelcostamesa.com/blog/2017/project-time-off-get-work-planning-vacation

CHAPTER 5
1. https://www.guideposts.org/better-living/travel/3-ways-to-shift-into-a-vacation-mindset
2. https://hbr.org/2015/06/get-in-the-right-state-of-mind-for-vacation
3. https://www.yogajournal.com/lifestyle/take-time-out
4. https://www.travelagentcentral.com/running-your-business/stats-stress-causing-37-percent-travelers-to-cancel-or-delay-vacation
5. https://www.bourncreative.com/how-to-take-a-real-vacation-even-if-you-own-a-business/
6. http://miamiherald.typepad.com/worklifebalancingact/2015/08/how-to-return-from-vacation.html
7. https://matadornetwork.com/notebook/8-ways-to-manage-pre-trip-anxiety/
8. https://www.linkedin.com/pulse/how-reduce-pre-vacation-stress-gloria-haboucha/
9. https://www.itmplatform.com/en/blog/5-pre-vacation-stress-busting-tips-for-project-managers/

CHEPTER 6
1. https://thepointsguy.com/2015/11/planning-a-vacation-1-6-months-out/
2. https://www.vacation-lists.com/3-months-before-vacation.html
3. http://www.telegraph.co.uk/travel/family-holidays/Holiday-planning-guide-12-steps-to-a-stress-free-break/
4. https://www.webmd.com/balance/stress-management/features/4-tips-to-reduce-vacation-stress#1
5. https://lifehacker.com/5923155/the-start-to-finish-guide-to-a-perfect-stress-free-vacation
6. https://hbr.org/2015/06/going-on-vacation-doesnt-have-to-stress-you-out-at-work

CHEPTER 7
1. http://corporette.com/how-to-delegate/
2. http://realtormag.realtor.org/tool-kit/personal-assistant/article/tasks-delegate-assistant
3. https://www.inc.com/david-finkel/27-things-to-delegate-to-your-assistant-to-make-your-life-smoother-faster-and-be.html
4. https://paysimple.com/blog/how-to-delegate-your-way-to-a-much-needed-vacation/
5. https://www.forbes.com/sites/martinzwilling/2013/10/02/how-to-delegate-more-effectively-in-your-business/#775583bf69bc
6. https://www.inc.com/jayson-demers/7-strategies-to-delegate-better-and-get-more-done.html
7. http://www.foxbusiness.com/features/the-ceos-secret-weapon-a-strong-executive-assistant

CHEPTER 8
1. https://projects.ncsu.edu/project/parkprgrd/PSTrainingModules/delegating/delsec1.htm
2. https://www.halogensoftware.com/blog/5-reasons-managers-need-to-delegate
3. http://leadertoday.org/faq/skillsdelegate.htm
4. https://www.shrm.org/resourcesandtools/hr-topics/organizational-and-employee-development/pages/delegateeffectively.aspx
5. http://www.telegraph.co.uk/connect/better-business/leadership/how-to-delegate-and-why-its-important/
6. https://hbr.org/2012/07/why-arent-you-delegating
7. https://www.forbes.com/sites/martinzwilling/2013/10/02/how-to-delegate-more-effectively-in-your-business/#775583bf69bc
8. https://www.forbes.com/sites/cywakeman/2015/08/25/dreading-delegation-why-its-more-vital-to-leadership-than-you-may-think/#42b64de82908
9. https://www.thebalance.com/delegation-101-for-small-business-owners-2951541
10. https://www.huffingtonpost.com/diane-gottsman/5-things-to-do-before-lea_b_7671704.html
11. https://www.inc.com/sean-stein-smith/4-tips-to-help-you-actually-relax-on-your-next-vacation.html
12. https://smallbiztrends.com/2014/07/employee-vacation-time-preparation.html

CHEPTER 9
1. http://www.youngadultmoney.com/2013/02/06/15-tips-for-planning-a-vacation/
2. http://traveltips.usatoday.com/prepare-vacation-1749.html
3. https://www.forbes.com/sites/jacquelynsmith/2013/06/24/how-to-take-a-stress-free-vacation-from-your-stressful-job-2/#370ffa3179a9
4. http://www.huffingtonpost.co.uk/entry/stress-free-vacation-prepare_n_3518955
5. http://www.smead.com/Director.aspx?NodeId=1740
6. https://www.huffingtonpost.com/elizabeth-grace-saunders/comprehensive-travel-checklist_b_5224092.html
7. https://www.monster.com/career-advice/article/steps-before-taking-vacation-from-work
8. https://www.fastcompany.com/3061919/3-essentials-steps-to-take-at-work-before-leaving-for-vacation
9. https://www.careeraddict.com/7-things-to-do-at-work-before-you-go-on-vacation
10. https://theundercoverrecruiter.com/going-on-holidays/

CHEPTER 10
1. http://www.youngadultmoney.com/2013/02/06/15-tips-for-planning-a-vacation/

2. https://redbooth.com/blog/how-to-delegate-tasks-while-vacationing
3. https://www.forbes.com/sites/kathryndill/2014/07/24/how-to-clear-your-mind-and-your-inbox-and-actually-take-a-vacation/#4da4eaca27fe
4. http://www.brainstorminc.com/blog/id/10254/how-to-actually-leave-work-behind-on-your-next-vacation
5. https://www.huffingtonpost.com/diane-gottsman/5-things-to-do-before-lea_b_7671704.html
6. https://www.huffingtonpost.com/elizabeth-grace-saunders/comprehensive-travel-checklist_b_5224092.html
7. https://www.monster.com/career-advice/article/steps-before-taking-vacation-from-work
8. http://www.businessinsider.com/8-things-to-do-at-work-before-your-next-vacation-2014-4?IR=T
9. https://www.careeraddict.com/7-things-to-do-at-work-before-you-go-on-vacation
10. http://thetraveltype.com/work-before-vacation/

CHEPTER 11

1. http://www.activebeat.com/your-health/8-reasons-to-do-a-digital-detox-in-2016/
2. https://www.itstimetologoff.com/2016/10/12/5-ways-a-digital-detox-benefits-your-mental-health/
3. https://www.forbes.com/sites/francesbooth/2015/02/03/30-reasons-to-do-a-digital-detox/#424165d7d2fc
4. http://www.healthfitnessrevolution.com/top-10-health-benefits-digital-detox/
5. https://www.huffingtonpost.com/lori-osterberg/digital-detox_b_8361700.html
6. https://www.entrepreneur.com/article/247799
7. https://www.projecttimeoff.com/blog/commentary/why-you-shouldn%E2%80%99t-work-through-your-vacation-explained-gifs
8. http://www.profitguide.com/manage-grow/human-resources/why-you-should-stop-employees-from-working-on-vacation-106496
9. https://www.forbes.com/sites/tanyamohn/2014/02/28/take-a-vacation-its-good-for-productivity-and-the-economy-according-to-a-new-study/#536603af5a33

CHEPTER 12

1. https://www.fastcompany.com/3050645/how-to-make-coming-back-from-vacation-and-less-horrible
2. https://www.forbes.com/sites/kathryndill/2014/07/28/5-tips-for-getting-back-to-work-after-a-vacation/#4b1b79c76f0a
3. https://www.thekitchn.com/the-smartest-thing-i-do-to-make-coming-back-from-vacation-easier-246514
4. https://www.forbes.com/sites/kathryndill/2014/07/28/5-tips-for-getting-back-to-work-after-a-vacation/#7f6af41a6f0a
5. https://www.lifehack.org/articles/work/everyone-should-know-these-10-tips-before-returning-work-after-vacation.html?platform=hootsuite
6. https://www.topresume.com/career-advice/10-tips-for-returning-from-vacation-with-minimal-stress

www.ingramcontent.com/pod-product-compliance
Lightning Source LLC
Chambersburg PA
CBHW030504220526
45464CB00006B/2647

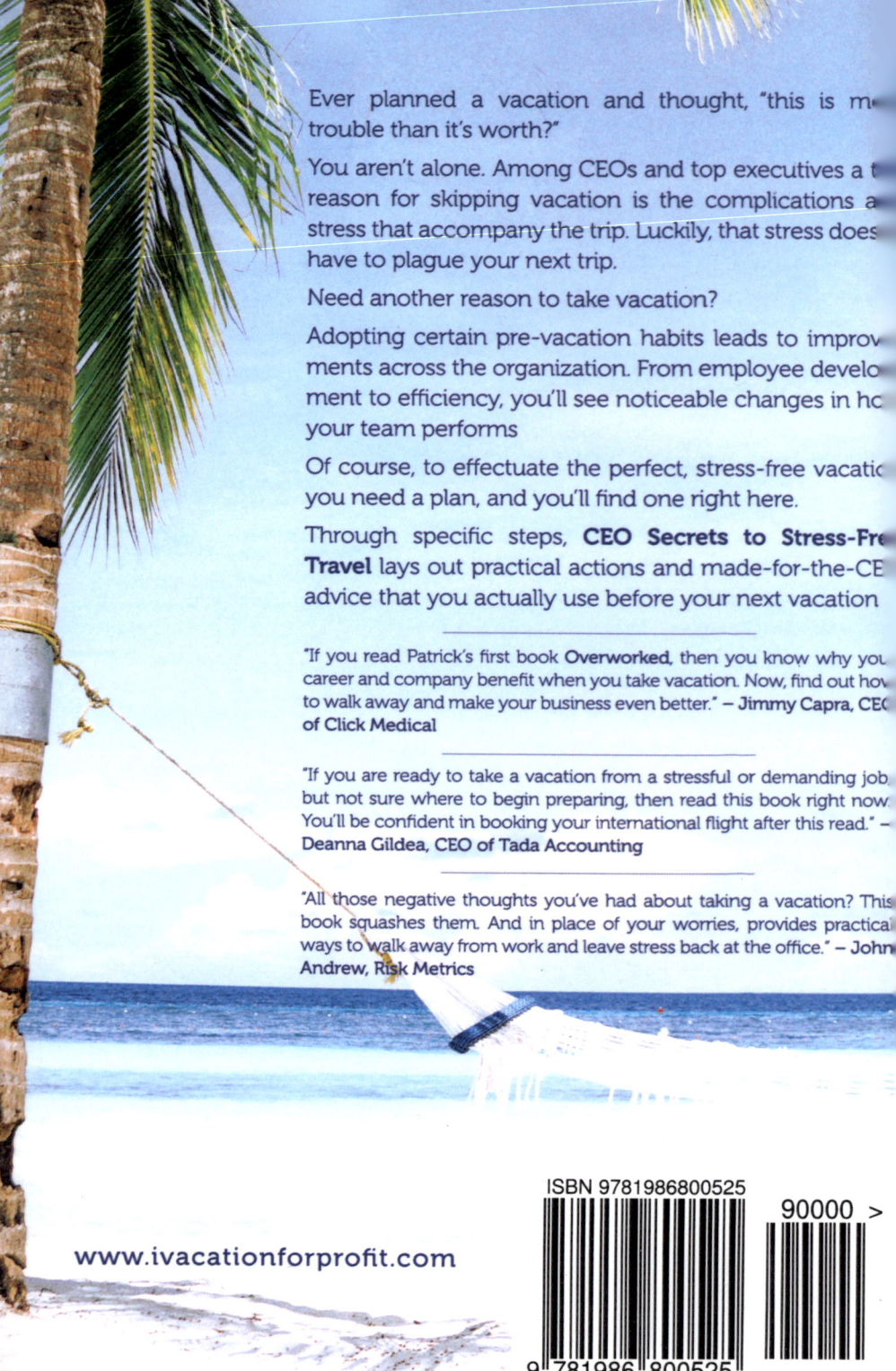

Ever planned a vacation and thought, "this is m[ore] trouble than it's worth?"

You aren't alone. Among CEOs and top executives a t[op] reason for skipping vacation is the complications a[nd] stress that accompany the trip. Luckily, that stress does[n't] have to plague your next trip.

Need another reason to take vacation?

Adopting certain pre-vacation habits leads to improv[e]ments across the organization. From employee develo[p]ment to efficiency, you'll see noticeable changes in ho[w] your team performs

Of course, to effectuate the perfect, stress-free vacatio[n] you need a plan, and you'll find one right here.

Through specific steps, **CEO Secrets to Stress-Fre[e] Travel** lays out practical actions and made-for-the-CE[O] advice that you actually use before your next vacation

"If you read Patrick's first book **Overworked**, then you know why you[r] career and company benefit when you take vacation. Now, find out ho[w] to walk away and make your business even better." – Jimmy Capra, CE[O] of Click Medical

"If you are ready to take a vacation from a stressful or demanding job, but not sure where to begin preparing, then read this book right now. You'll be confident in booking your international flight after this read." – Deanna Gildea, CEO of Tada Accounting

"All those negative thoughts you've had about taking a vacation? This book squashes them. And in place of your worries, provides practica[l] ways to walk away from work and leave stress back at the office." – John Andrew, Risk Metrics

www.ivacationforprofit.com

ISBN 9781986800525